Math All Around
Multiplication on the Farm

Jennifer Rozines Roy and Gregory Roy

Marshall Cavendish
Benchmark
New York

The sun is rising. The rooster crows. It's morning in the country.

Let's take a walk around the farm. As we do, we can find things to **multiply**.

When you multiply, you repeat a number over and over again until you get a larger number.

Put on your boots. We have some walking—and multiplying—to do!

First, let's visit the animals! The pigs are eating breakfast.

There are six bins with food in them. Three pigs are eating at each bin. How many pigs are there in all?

We could count them one at a time, but that would take a while. There are faster and easier ways to count larger numbers.

One way to count the pigs is by skip-counting. Skip-counting jumps over some numbers.

Let's skip-count by threes, because there are three pigs eating at each bin.

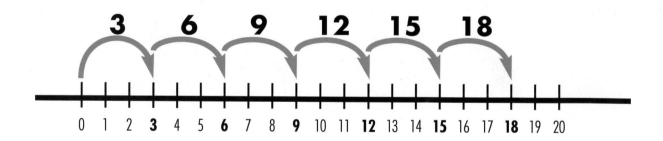

There are eighteen hungry pigs. They sure gobbled up their food fast. We counted fast, too, thanks to skip-counting.

Today is a special day for the horses on the farm. The **farrier** is coming to put new shoes on them.

There are eight horses. Each horse has four hooves. How many shoes will the farrier need?

We could add up all of the hooves by counting them one at a time. But the horses are moving around the field. It's hard to keep track of them. So let's skip-count by fours.

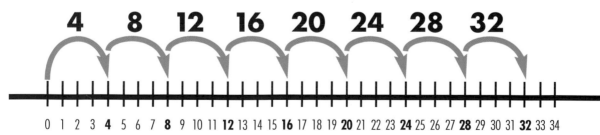

We skip-counted eight times for eight horses.

Four hooves times eight horses equals thirty-two shoes. If we write it as a **multiplication** fact, it looks like this:

4 hooves **x** **8** horses **=** **32** shoes

$$
\begin{array}{r}
4 \\
\times\ 8 \\
\hline
32
\end{array}
$$
←——*this line means "equals"*

The "x" is a symbol that means "times" or multiplied by.

The two numbers that are multiplied are called **factors**. Here, **4** and **8** are factors.

The answer in a multiplication fact is called the **product**. Here, **32** is the product.

The farrier will need thirty-two shiny new horseshoes for eight beautiful horses.

The chicken coop is where the hens lay their eggs. Today, they laid twelve eggs.

We can collect the eggs and make different multiplication facts with them.

First, place them in one row.

12 eggs **x 1** row **= 12** eggs

⬤⬤⬤⬤⬤⬤⬤⬤⬤⬤⬤⬤

$$\begin{array}{r} \mathbf{12} \\ \times\ \mathbf{1} \\ \hline \mathbf{12} \end{array}$$

Next, put them in two rows. There are six eggs in each row.

6 eggs **x 2** rows **= 12** eggs

⬤⬤⬤⬤⬤⬤
⬤⬤⬤⬤⬤⬤

$$\begin{array}{r} \mathbf{6} \\ \times\ \mathbf{2} \\ \hline \mathbf{12} \end{array}$$

How about three rows? Four eggs in each!

3 rows **x 4** eggs **= 12** eggs

$$\begin{array}{r} 3 \\ \times\ 4 \\ \hline 12 \end{array}$$

Now, try four rows. Three eggs in each!

4 rows **x 3** eggs **= 12** eggs

$$\begin{array}{r} 4 \\ \times\ 3 \\ \hline 12 \end{array}$$

Different factors can be multiplied together to get the same product.

The hens did good work laying eggs, and we did good work multiplying them.

Goats' milk can be used to make delicious cheese. If five nanny goats each give five **pints** of milk a day, how much milk is there for cheese?

We can find out by skip-counting.

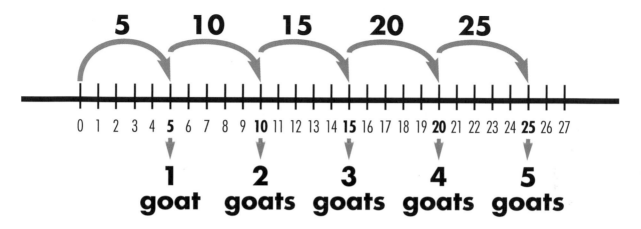

5   **10**   **15**   **20**   **25**

0 1 2 3 4 **5** 6 7 8 9 **10** 11 12 13 14 **15** 16 17 18 19 **20** 21 22 23 24 **25** 26 27

1
goat   **2**
goats   **3**
goats   **4**
goats   **5**
goats

So, five pints from five goats is twenty-five pints of milk.

5 pints   **x**   **5** goats   **=**   **25** pints

Twenty-five pints of goats' milk will make a lot of cheese!

Of course, goats aren't the only farm animals that make milk. Cows do, too!

On this farm, cows are milked the old-fashioned way—by hand. Each of these three cows makes about six **gallons** of milk a day.

Let's multiply.

3 cows **x 6** gallons **= ?** gallons

We can skip-count by threes six times:
3, 6, 9, 12, 15, 18.

$$3 \times 6 = 18$$

$$
\begin{array}{r}
3 \\
\times\ 6 \\
\hline
18
\end{array}
$$

What happens if we switch the two factors?

6 gallons **x 3** cows **= ?** gallons

We can skip-count by sixes three times:
6, 12, 18.

$$6 \times 3 = 18$$

$$
\begin{array}{r}
6 \\
\times\ 3 \\
\hline
18
\end{array}
$$

We get the same product. And plenty of fresh milk, too!

Farmers don't just raise animals. They also grow **crops**, like grains, fruits, and vegetables.

This farm has a small cornfield. The corn is planted in straight rows, with an equal number of cornstalks in each row.

How will we count all the cornstalks? First, we'll count the number of rows. Ten!

Next, let's walk along the outside edge and count how many stalks are in each row. There are ten stalks in each row.

Ten rows of ten stalks. Let's skip-count by tens: **10**, **20**, **30**, **40**, **50**, **60**, **70**, **80**, **90**, **100**!

10 rows **x 10** cornstalks **= 100** cornstalks

$$\begin{array}{r} \mathbf{10} \\ \mathbf{\times 10} \\ \hline \mathbf{100} \end{array}$$

In the garden, we pick some tomatoes to fill our two baskets. We put seven ripe, juicy tomatoes in each basket.

7 tomatoes **x 2** baskets **= 14** tomatoes

7 x 2 = 14

$$\begin{array}{r} 7 \\ \times\ 2 \\ \hline 14 \end{array}$$

Next, we put some peppers in another basket. Nine green peppers fit inside.

9 peppers **x 1** basket **= 9** peppers

9 x 1 = 9

$$\begin{array}{r} 9 \\ \times\ 1 \\ \hline 9 \end{array}$$

Let's carry the baskets to the farmhouse. The farmer will be happy to see the good food fresh from the garden!

Just outside the farmhouse there are some dishes. Who eats and drinks from these? The farm cats! Three cats live on the farm. Here they come for breakfast. Let's feed them.

There is one water dish for each cat.

$$\begin{array}{r} 1 \\ \times\ 3 \\ \hline 3 \end{array}$$

1 water dish **x 3** cats **= 3** water dishes

1 x 3 = 3

Each cat also gets a food dish.

$$\begin{array}{r} 3 \\ \times\ 1 \\ \hline 3 \end{array}$$

3 cats **x 1** food dish **= 3** food dishes

3 x 1 = 3

And each cat gets two treats.

3 cats **x 2** treats **= 6** treats

3 x 2 = 6

$$\begin{array}{r} 3 \\ \times\ 2 \\ \hline 6 \end{array}$$

Everybody gets plenty to eat and drink.

Come into the farmhouse. It's time for *our* breakfast. Meals on the farm are fresh and tasty.

There are five people at the table. Each person gets one glass of milk, two eggs, three slices of bacon, one piece of toast, and four cubes of cheese. How much food is on the table?

5 people **x 2** eggs **= 10** eggs

$$\begin{array}{r} 5 \\ \times\ 2 \\ \hline 10 \end{array}$$

5 people **x 3** slices of bacon **= 15** slices of bacon

$$\begin{array}{r} 5 \\ \times\ 3 \\ \hline 15 \end{array}$$

5 people **x 1** piece of toast **= 5** pieces of toast

$$\begin{array}{r} 5 \\ \times\ 1 \\ \hline 5 \end{array}$$

5 people **x 4** cubes of cheese **= 20** cubes of cheese

$$\begin{array}{r} 5 \\ \times\ 4 \\ \hline 20 \end{array}$$

5 people **x 1** glass of milk **= 5** glasses of milk

$$\begin{array}{r} 5 \\ \times\ 1 \\ \hline 5 \end{array}$$

25

It takes hard work to grow crops and provide enough food for a family. Multiplication makes understanding farming a little easier.

How do you use multiplication in *your* life?

Glossary

crops—Farm products, such as corn, that are grown in the soil.

factor—A number that is multiplied by another number.

farrier—A person who puts shoes on horses.

gallon—A unit of measure for liquids that is equal to four quarts or eight pints.

multiplication—The act of adding a number to itself a certain number of times to get a product.

multiply—To add a number to itself a certain number of times to get a product.

pint—A unit of volume that is equal to a half quart.

product—The number you get when you multiply two or more numbers.

Read More

Clemson, Wendy. *Times Tables!* DK Children, 2001.

Fowler, Allan. *Rookie Read-About Geography: Living on Farms.* Children's Press, 2000.

Mills, Claudia. *7 x 9 = Trouble!* Farrar, Straus and Giroux, 2002.

Web Sites

AAAKnow Math: Multiplication
www.aaaknow.com/mul.htm

A+ Math
www.aplusmath.com

United States Department of Agriculture (USDA)
www.usda.gov

Index

Page numbers in **boldface** are illustrations.

About the Authors

Jennifer Rozines Roy is the author of more than twenty books. A former Gifted and Talented teacher, she holds degrees in psychology and elementary education.

Gregory Roy is a civil engineer who has co-authored several books with his wife. The Roys live in upstate New York with their son Adam.

Marshall Cavendish Benchmark
99 White Plains Road
Tarrytown, New York 10591-9001
www.marshallcavendish.us

Library of Congress Cataloging-in-Publication Data

Roy, Jennifer Rozines, 1967–
Multiplication on the farm / by Jennifer Rozines Roy & Gregory Roy.
p. cm. — (Math all around)
Summary: "Reinforces both multiplication and reading skills, stimulates critical thinking,
and provides students with an understanding of math in the real world"—Provided by publisher.
Includes index.
ISBN-13: 978-0-7614-2268-6
ISBN-10: 0-7614-2268-4
1. Multiplication—Juvenile literature. 2. Thought and thinking—Study and teaching (Elementary)—Activity programs—Juvenile literature.
3. Farm life—Juvenile literature. I. Roy, Gregory. II. Title.
III. Series: Roy, Jennifer Rozines, 1967– Math all around.
QA115.R686 2006
513.2'13—dc22
2006009168

Photo Research by Anne Burns Images

Cover Photo by *Animals Animals*/Jim Steinberg

The photographs in this book are used with permission and through the courtesy of:
Corbis: pp. 1, 16 Macduff Everton; p. 16(inset) Paul Gun; p. 18(inset) J. Westrich/zefa; p. 18 Jim Craigmyle; p. 23L&R DK Limited.
Superstock: p. 2 Digital Vision; p. 5 Superstock; pp. 8, 21B Brand X; p. 11 Comstock; p. 12T Piktal; pp. 12B, 13 Medio Images;
p. 15 age fotostock; p. 20 Food Collection; pp. 21T, 25(Row2) Ingram Publishing Ingram Publishing; pp. 24R, 25(Row5)
BananaStock; p. 26 RubberBall. *Animals Animals*: p. 7 Michael S. Bisceglie; p. 9 Bob Langrish; p. 14 Michael Gadomski;
p. 23C Lynn O'Dell. *Jay Mallin*: pp. 22(all), 24L, 25(Row1,3,4).

Series design by Virginia Pope

Printed in Malaysia
3 5 6 4 2